JACOBEAN EMBROIDERY,
ITS FORMS AND FILLINGS
INCLUDING LATE TUDOR

GW00645600

Jacobean Embroidery

Its Forms and Fillings
Including Late Tudor

BY

ADA WENTWORTH FITZWILLIAM

AND

A. F. MORRIS HANDS

B. T. Batsford Ltd, London

© Ada Wentworth Fitzwilliam & A. F. Morris Hands, 1928
First paperback edition 1990

ISBN 0 7134 6376 7

Printed and bound in Hong Kong
For the Publishers
B. T. Batsford Ltd
4 Fitzhardinge Street
London W1H 0AH

CONTENTS

Introductory History by A. F. Morris Hands.

LIST OF ILLUSTRATIONS

LIST OF ILLUSTRATIONS

INTRODUCTION

TO redeem the monotony of plain surfaces has ever been the aim of all the arts, but especially that of the needle, which being the oldest expression of decorative intention, has, from the earliest time, been very dependent on its groundwork for its ultimate results. This is particularly the case in embroideries of the type of what is commonly known as Jacobean, where the ground fabric is extensively visible, as it is also in that wondrous achievement, the Bayeux tapestry worked in coarse wools upon homespun linen and therefore quite miscalled " tapestry."

Inaccuracy in nomenclature is one of the stumbling blocks the student encounters, and the tendency of the day to classify " styles " by the restricted formula of monarchical periods is likewise misleading. No style is ever solely distinctive of one reign, or even one century, the law of evolution rules the arts as it does nature, there is always a correlation between styles in art and circumstances of existence that is productive of gradual changes of taste, therefore, pronounced evidences in design are, actually, the culminating point in a course of combined influences which have reached the period of individual expression.

Crewel work of the type of Jacobean, was the outcome of that earlier wool embroidery that even in the zenith of fame of the Ecclesiastical broderers still quietly went on its way.

In the middle ages, furnishing of rooms was scanty, and embroidered hangings, cushion and stool covers provided the necessary notes of colour and comfort; the wall hangings of the 13th century were of coarse canvas decorated with a design executed in wools.

It is curious how in English embroideries there has always been a predilection on the part of the designers for interlacing stems, and for the inconsequent introduction of birds and beasts.

Mons de Farcy, author of *La Broderie du Onzième siecle jusqu' à nos jours*, remarks that "it seems that the position of England, surrounded by the sea on all sides, has provoked in its inhabitants the passion of travelling over the sea, and they came to know, before continental nations, of the parrots and other birds of brilliant plumage so often reproduced in their needlework."*

Mrs. Christie, an English authority on Embroidery, admirably sums up the evolution of designs when she writes "Examination of old Embroideries gathered from all parts of the world

*Opus Anglicum by M. Louis de Farcy in "Embroidery"

shows that each individual specimen, every flower and bud, is a development of some existing form, and is not an original creation, invented, as some appear to think all designs are, upon the spur of the moment." In the creation of a design it is a case of assimilation of the fittest and the elimination of the unsuitable from existing examples, thus the interlacing stems of the work of the 14th century became grafted on to the version of the Tree of Life idea in the Oriental designs that came to England in the 16th, through the intercourse opened up by the formation of the East India Company, at the end of Elizabeth's reign.

To deem, as do some writers, the bold, rather ponderous crewel work of the 17th century, sole outcome of the importation of the Palampores of Musulipatan, is to ignore all the tendencies manifested in the embroideries of previous centuries; in the same way, to repudiate the emblematical significance of special features markedly introduced into old designs, is to betray a complete lack of knowledge of the mind and manners of the people of superstitious days.

Knowledge was not rapidly acquired, and even as late as the 17th century was largely disseminated through the country by allegorical narratives, while emblematical lore reflected the history of the immediate moment. There was in the poetry and in the embroidery of Elizabeth's day, a sportive quality which was not likely to be checked under the Stuarts, *doubles entendres* were not confined to jests! and the political and religious differences of opinion, rampant throughout the period, found expression in the most fantastic ways.

The Stump Embroidery, in vogue at the same time as the crewel hangings specially treated in this volume, was full of symbolism, and naturally the same inspiration directed the worker in crewels. Curiously enough, both these very different types of needlework, crystalised into individuality concurrently, yet one is usually designated Jacobean, the other referred to as Stuart. In this connection it is well also to remember, that the Stuart era extended, historically, from 1603 to 1714, *viz.*, from the reign of James I (Jacobus) to that of Queen Anne, daughter of James II.

Queen Anne is so often relegated, in the public mind, to an isolated position, genealogically, and the pronounced developments in the changes of taste that took place at the commencement of the of the 18th century, left such a very definite impression, that she is rarely remembered as a Stuart; it was in her reign, however, that the vogue for the old crewel embroideries revived, and though differences of treatment crept in, the designs, were, in the main, purely Jacobean, being copies or adaptations of patterns popular in the middle of the 17th century. It is these copies that exist mostly to-day, few, indeed, are those hangings which pertain to the earlier date, but a study of those few, taken in conjunction with the still fewer that remain of the 16th century, prove the *gradual* growth of the designs that have the tree motif which makes them all kin.

Lady Brougham and Vaux had a most wonderful collection, from which interesting comparisons could be made. One pair of bed hangings, of coarse linen of the 16th century, show the trees with a meandering growth entirely characteristic of those of heavier kind which appear in later embroideries, these trees also are undoubtedly intended to represent the Tree of Life, for round one is coiled a serpent, while beneath the scanty but large leaved boughs, incidents in the story of the expulsion from Paradise are to be descried, as also the procession into the ark.

The work is without doubt early, for there is a primitive character in the arrangement of the inconsequent groups of figures, Adam and Eve stand nude either side the tree, couples in weird though contemporaneous costume to the work are dotted over the surface quite at haphazard.

The similarity between the tree on these curtains and on one of the 18th century once in the same collection is very striking. Added grace of design has beautified the later work, but the same forms can be traced and the same parrots and squirrels are introduced, the Biblical story at the foot of the 16th century curtain has been replaced by a portion of the legend of the human soul.

Another very interesting example I have seen, attributed to the years of James I's reign, seems to suggest that the worker had realised the "waves" in an Eastern pattern and made growths of coral at the base of the tree, but had then converted a line or two of waves into *terra firma*, for at one end reposes a lion, towards which a stag is bounding with head turned back as if in fear of pursuers.

The birds in this example are very tropical, a miniature peacock on the lower branches spreads its tail stiffly, parrots like the one illustrated in our collection of details, birds of paradise, and squirrels, are all to be noted among foliations that are the most superb, taken individually, it is possible to imagine, most are worked fairly solid, such light fillings as there are, being small sprays of leaves like those in our plate No. 17.

Carnations, harebells, canterbury bells, roses, marigolds, grapes, are included in the composition; block shading, chain stitch, stem stitch are all employed in the working, and a very interesting example of the Opus Plumarian is given in the tail feathers of the tiny peacock.

The dissection of detail in early English crewel embroidery is a very fascinating occupation and well repays the expenditure of time. So little has been written about this particular phase of the embroiderer's art, that it is by old records and examples one becomes best informed and in a great measure enabled to trace the growth of the style that culminated in the massive designs that derived their name from the epoch in which they were in favour. Tudor crewel work, was chiefly done in broad outline of a more or less fanciful nature as regards the stitching, witness the sections of that Tudor piece which is shewn in our first illustration.

Forms were large but gradually became reduced as they were worked more solidly. The beautiful foxglove pattern in "Bess of Hardwicke's" curtains at Hardwicke, shews a very slight feeling of transition but it may safely be assumed that one of the influences bearing on the execution of the crewel work, was the portentous character of much of the contemporary canvas hand-worked tapestry such as the famous set of panels unearthed in Hatton Gardens. The architectural basis is a link between the Ecclesiastical and Secular embroideries of the past centuries, and anyone interested in the evolution of design would be struck with the similitude of the large leaves and flowers in these panels to those of the crewel designs of the same date; it is also noteworthy that the symbolic significance in the details of the panels is ecclesiastic, whereas in the crewel work it is always based on the legend of the Tree of Life, or secularly emblematic.

Colourings were often in both styles, blues, greens, bright yellows and browns predominated, carnation reds figuring in some examples, used for the flower of that name and for the pomegranate, which, with its seeds visible, signifies future life and immortality.

The carnation and the caterpillar were both Stuart emblems, and occur in nearly all kinds of work executed during their reigns; the rose, of course, has its national as well as its religious significance, likewise the oak (after the restoration).

The potato flower seen in both Jacobean and Portuguese embroideries is an example of the habit of recording the latest novelty, the strawberry was also popular on this account, and is frequently introduced in those hillocky foregrounds, which, to me, appear one of the most interesting evidences of combined influences.

Once again, another Oriental idea was evidently assimilated, for in numberless Chinese patterns one sees the main motive springing out of a base of waves formed exactly like the hillocks which became such a distinctive feature in these large branching designs.

In the earliest examples the hillocks were much broken up, and smaller (more like the mounds in the painted Palampores) than in the later work, from which we may presume the spread of the Oriental influence had done its work, the " terra firma " being carried out with a similitude to the eastern version of waves that includes the actual stitchery; grafted on to this was the legend of the pursuit of the human soul (typified by a hart) by evil, personified by the huntsman, the hounds and various uncanny beasts, two bearing unflattering resemblance to the heraldic lion and leopard; while rabbits, snails, grubs of all kind hinder the hart's progress, these are relics of the days when The Bestiarta (symbolism of beasts) was carefully studied.

The riotous re-action from the Puritan rule was reflected in the embroideries of the restoration, as in everything else, and patterns became exuberant, colouring more brilliant, the exquisite stitchery gradually gave place to the easier achievement of solid fillings, and the requisite relief was secured by light sprays filling up the ground between the larger leaves, jasmine, cherries, harebells, potato flowers, honeysuckle, shamrock or trefoil and acorns took the lead.

It is an almost impossible task to describe the large leaves, since they bear no resemblance to anything natural, they are, however, rarely angular in outline, rejoicing rather in sweeping curves, and drooping points, curled over to display the under side of the leaf, a device that gave opening for much ingenuity in the arrangement of the stitches. The variety in these was so great that on reading the enumeration made by Taylor, the Water Poet, one becomes quite breathless. The predominating ones, however, are—*Outline or Stem Stitch*, used for all but the largest stems, and veining and outlining leaves and flowers.

Shading Stitch, sometimes called long and short, used for large branches and leaves, *Basket* and *Double Back Stitch* are also used for these stems.

Satin Stitch, for all kinds of flowers and small foliage, or for the definite flat shading, that is like block shading without the ridge caused by the carrying back of the wool into the past row of stitches.

Buttonhole, also much used for leaves, especially those having light fillings and broad outlines.

Rope Stitch, *Coral*, *Cable* and *Chain*, also for outlines, the last named being also used for fillings.

The fancy fillings such as darning, French knots, etc., are demonstrated and described in the following pages, and the colour plates endeavour to give the idea of the correct colourings. In this connection, a few observations, based on the study of genuine originals, may not be amiss.

As I have before mentioned, a certain brilliancy characterised the work at one period, but this cannot be regarded as the best type to imitate. The most harmonius were carried out in two schemes. One had all the leaves worked in Mandarin blues, shading from darkest indigo to softest blue-grey. These were placed in juxtaposition, with tender mignonette and silvery greens, a strong accent being *occasionally* introduced by a flower or filling carried out in true rose leaf shade or by veinings of bronze greens and browns.

The other scheme, and this is more rarely met with, was in bronze greens throughout, intermixed with yellow and about three shades of the dull blues. Black sometimes is to be noticed in both these colour schemes, also bright and buff yellows and chestnut browns, and the colours were mostly confined to the blue scheme first named, but there are examples extant of an entire design carried out in shades of red, as in the Tudor and early 16th century hangings one finds blues responsible for the whole colouring. These vary in tone, and in the late copies of the designs the blue has a very green tinge about it.*

In the reign of Queen Anne taste reverted to the older lighter designs, grotesques were eliminated, massiveness gave place to grace, and brightness of colour to a soft modified brilliancy that was very engaging. In the Georgian copies heaviness again obtained favour, and gradually the designs deteriorated, and were eventually temporarily lost in "the limbo of the past." The vogue for lace work in the reign of William and Mary influenced the stitches in the crewel embroidery, and in Queen Anne's day the variety of stitches was reminiscent of the earlier period, some of the fillings being beautiful.

The material used was through all the phases the same, viz., a twill fabric, of which the warp was of linen, the weft of cotton; the wools varied somewhat in the twist, but were always worsted, the word crewel being a diminutive of clew, "a ball of thread," and probably came into vogue with the importation of wools from Germany, the corresponding word in that language being *Knäuel.*

A. F. MORRIS HANDS

* See example in South Kensington carried out in very hard twisted blue wools. The curtain belonging to Mr. Hearn, and now at South Kensington, is a beautiful specimen of the full colouring of the late 17th century.

Op. I

PLATE I

THIS plate was sketched from a very old strip of Tudor work, measuring about 5ft. 8in. in length and 1ft. 8in. in width. Each leaf was about 22in. long and 19in. across. The strip had evidently been part of a bed valance, and, as far as one could tell—for it was much faded—had been worked in two shades of wool only—dark indigo blue and bright green ; the latter had faded, almost everywhere, to a soft mignonette colour.

1

Op. II

PLATE 2

GROUP of blue leaves, etc., taken from some old cushions at Knole Park, Sevenoaks.

No. 1. Stem stitch contour: Maidenhair in button-hole stitch. Star in buttonhole stitch on background of small crosses.

No. 2. Stem stitch.

No. 3. Stem stitch contours. Centre in loop stitch.

No. 4. Stem stitch contours. Centre loop stitch and maidenhair in buttonhole stitch.

No. 5. Stem stitch.

Op. II

PLATE 2

Op. II

PLATE 2a

GROUP of the lighter details that break up the heavy masses in the earliest and latest examples.

The medlar-like fruit is worked in Crewel stitch in bands of brown, stem lighter in shade.

The leaves, Example I & II, satin stitch with stem stitch outline both sides, centre veinings in stem stitch, turnover in leaf, II, in block stitch.

III Buttonhole edging with darned centre, centre filled with strands of wool caught down at intervals with double back stitch.

IV Flowers in soft blues in satin stitch, acorns have their cups worked in French knots.

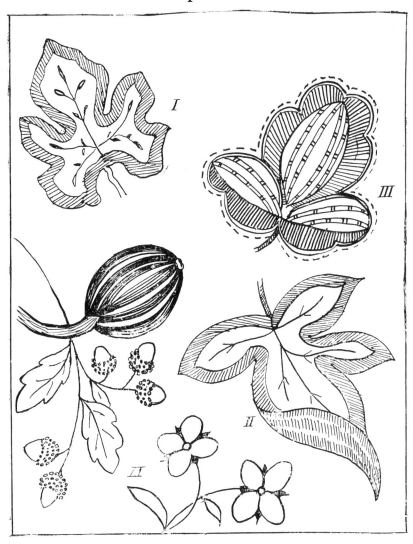

PLATE 2a

Op. III

THE following plates were sketched from an old strip of work done in deep indigo worsted wool, with a rather lighter wool, both in colour and make, used in the fine buttonhole work and darning, of which there is much throughout the work. The design was a branching one, the flowers and leaves—most of which appear in the following plates—are hanging from stems about a quarter of an inch thick done in herring-bone stitch, with the exception of the violas (plate 5) which have a thicker stem of their own in herring-bone, stem stitch and loops. The thistles (plate 3, No. 1) reproduced the same size as in the work, were scattered about in groups of three, making a very pleasing contrast to the hanging roses (plate 6), whilst the irises reared their heads all along the bottom of the strip, but owing to the work having been cut, it was impossible to see how they joined their straight stalks to the branching ones above.

PLATE 3

No. 1. Stem stitch contour: diaper work done in coral stitch, with a French knot filling in each alternate square. Four rows of buttonhole stitch at top of flower.

No. 2. Stem-stitch, coral stitch and darning.

No. 3. Buttonhole stitch, French knot and stem stitch.

No. 4. Stem stitch and buttonhole stitch.

No. 5. Coral stitch. (These tendrils occurred all over the work and were very effective.)

No. 6. Buttonhole stitch: centre and stalk in stem stitch.

No. 7. Stem stitch and loops.

Op. III

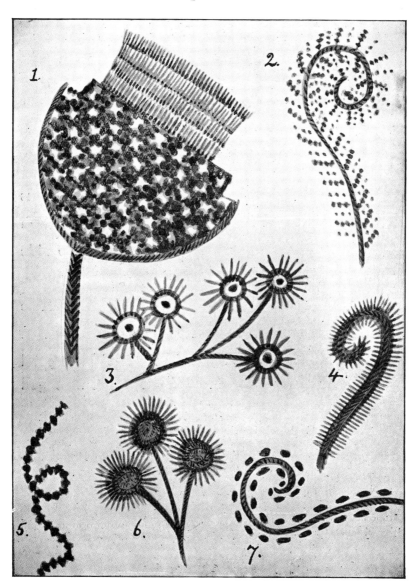

PLATE 3

Op. III

PLATE 4

THE iris shown here was worked as follows : The contours in stem stitch throughout. The centre and two side petals have stem stitch veins, edged buttonhole stitch and were filled in with big knots. The smaller petals were partially filled in with buttonhole stitch and darning. The dark petal on left was done in Cretan* stitch edged stem stitch.

* A variation of herring bone stitch.

8

Op. III

PLATE 4

Op. 114

PLATE 5

No. 1. Contour in stem stitch, filled in lightly with buttonhole stitch, and darning and long-and-short stitch.

No. 2. Ditto, with the addition of herring-bone stitch on two upper petals.

No. 3. (Stalk) herring-bone stem stitch with loops between.

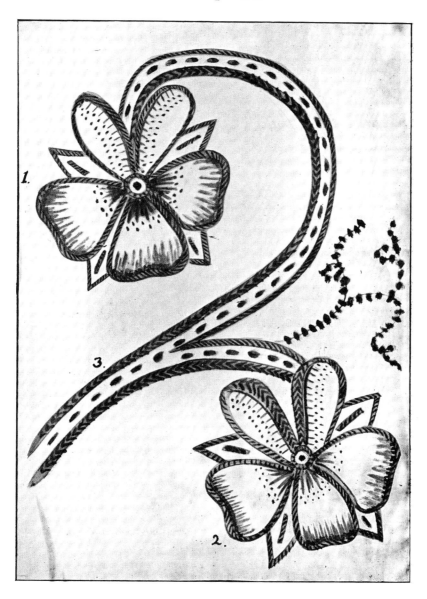

PLATE 5

Op. III

PLATE 6

No. 1. Stem-stitch, buttonhole stitch and darning.

No. 2. Ditto.

No. 3. Stem stitch, buttonhole stitch, French knots and darning.

No. 4. Stem stitch, buttonhole stitch and darning.

All have herring-bone stitch stalks.

Sketched from a piece of work in blue crewels on white linen, (belonged to the late Lady Maria Ponsonby).

Op. III

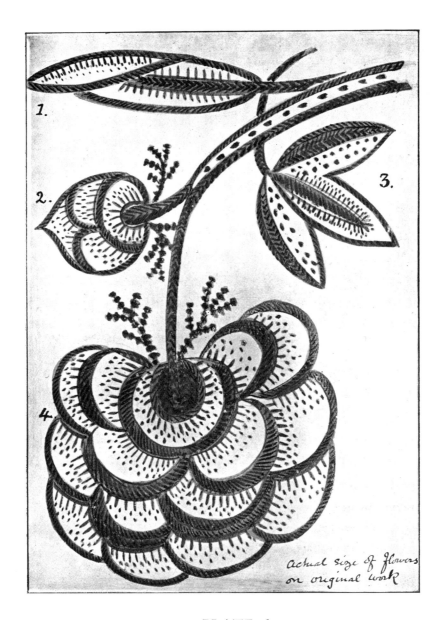

1.
2.
3.
4.

Actual size of flowers on original work

PLATE 6

Op. III

PLATE 7

MOST of the stitchery shown here is similar to that on the preceding plates, but has the addition of the plait stitch* edged with buttonhole stitch in the veins of the big leaf, and the close knots on the sheaf of the foxgloves, while the sheaf of the convolvulus has veins of stem stitch and small French knots.

In all this piece of work there is to be noted a great deal of buttonholing and darning.

---

*A variation of herring-bone stitch.

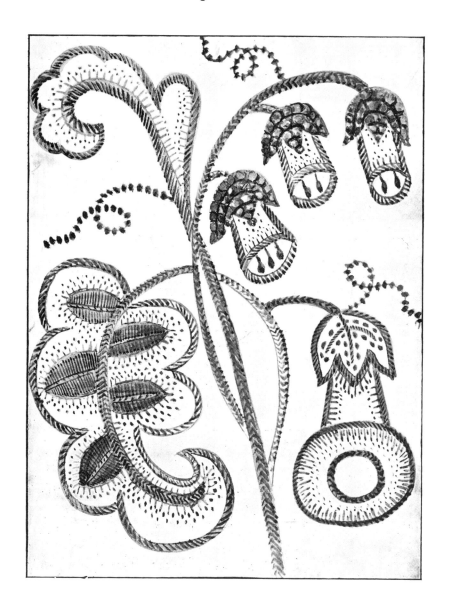

PLATE 7

Op. IV

PLATE 8

SHOWS many uses to which stem stitch can be put, being the only stitch employed in the work illustrated here, if we except the little arrow-heads used to edge the vine leaf.

Op. IV

DATED AD 1696

A.W.F

PLATE 8

Op. IV

THE following sketches were taken from a most beautiful and elaborate strip of work, forming part of some bed-hangings, dated A.D. 1696, worked in hard twisted crewels in blue, mignonette, and green colourings only.

PLATE 9

treats of button-holeing stitch done in a variety of ways.

No. 1 has groups of three button-hole stitches and crosses in centre, and is edged by chain stitch and arrow-heads.

No. 2. Button-hole stitch centre and edge.

No. 3. Button-hole stitch with stalks in stem stitch.

PLATE 9

Op. IV

PLATE 10

N this sketch are three principal stitches, viz.: Chain stitch filling in spaces Nos. 1-2 (on left of sketch) and forming the contour of the whole leaf; button-hole stitch filling spaces Nos. 3-4; and a lace stitch filling spaces Nos. 5-6-7. The other two spaces are filled by brick stitch, and darning with little veins of coral stitch and herring bone. There are loop stitches in the centre of the veining in spaces 6-7, and these are also worked round the outside of the leaf.

Op. IV

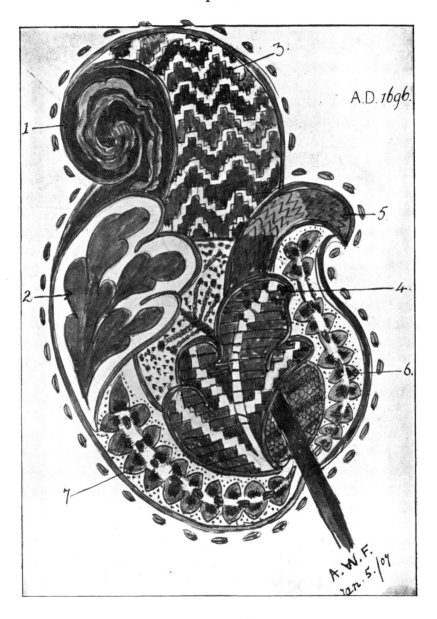

PLATE 10

Op. IV

PLATE 10*a*

THIS leaf, having a contour of chain stitch, is filled in at the top with a brown and blue branch in stem stitch, edged with short-and-long stitch. The green turnover is in chain stitch with blue chain stitch veins, and the blue turnovers at base of leaf are done in a lace surface stitch, while the rest is filled in with small darning stitches, coral stitches and a little bit of button-hole stitching. The three central leaves crossing stem are in red and green, and blue and green; the brown stalks are worked in stem stitch. Loops are worked round the outside of the leaf here as in all the bigger leaves on this work. The spike on the left of the sketch is in herring bone stitch edged with arrow heads.

Op. IV

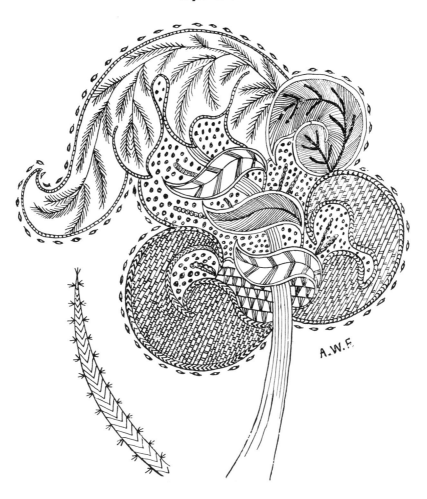

PLATE 10*a*

Op. V

THE following three plates are sketches from the bed hangings in the "Chapel" room at Hardwicke Hall, Derbyshire— the property of the Duke of Devonshire.

PLATE 11

Shows the full design, which is a repeating one, of the hangings. The details of the stitchery will be found on the following plates.

Op. V

PLATE 11

Op. V

PLATE 12

No. 1. One of the many conventional foliations in this design, carried out in stem stitch, buttonhole and darning.

No. 2. Close chain stitch for the circles with herring bone for the stalk running through them.

No. 3. The same stem as in foxgloves but with darning introduced up the centre.

No. 4. The sheafs of the foxgloves are worked in crochet stitch edged stem stitch.

The contours of flowers in back stitch, filled in short-and-long stitches and darning.

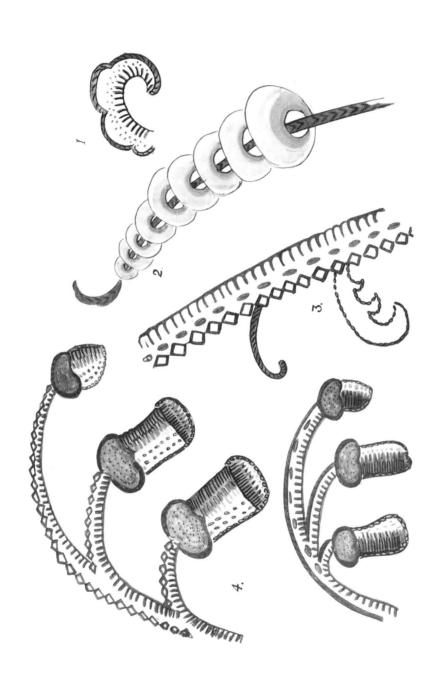

1.

2.

3.

4.

Op. V

PLATE 13

No. 1. Contour in chain stitch. Vein stem stitch edged two rows short-and-long stitches and darning.

No. 2. Contour in *double* chain stitch. Veins in knot stitch edged darning. Loops in middle of centre vein.

No. 3. Contour in stem stitch; vein ditto, edged with two rows of short-and-long stitches and darning.

No. 4. Contour in chain stitch, edged darning. Centre vein chain stitch. Branching veins knot stitch outlined with darning stitches.

No. 5. Contour buttonhole stitch and darning. Veins knot stitch and darning.

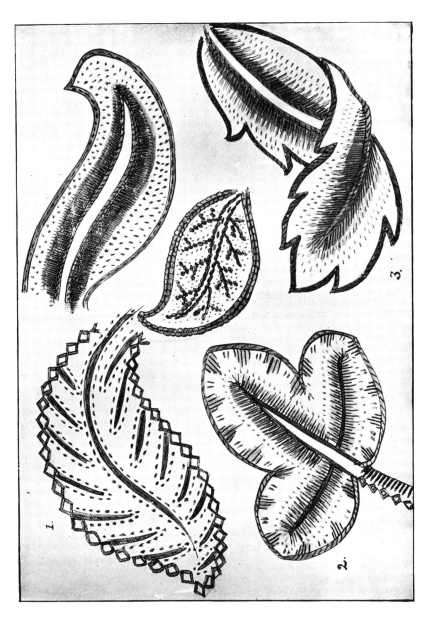

PLATE 13

Op. V*a*

PLATE 14

A GROUP of fillings in which darning plays an important part, the backgrounds of two of the leaves were carried out in indigo, the veinings were worked in solid rows of outline stitch in brown shading to a lighter bronze green, the central vein in the upper leaf was in chain-stitch in dark blue and the outline of leaf was carried out in two rows of chain stitching in darkest indigo. The shamrock leaf has a darned contour of double threads, the filling was in stem stitch, solid, with bars of a darker colour worked across it. The little band at the bottom of the group was a mixture of satin, chain, stem and French knots.

Op. V*a*

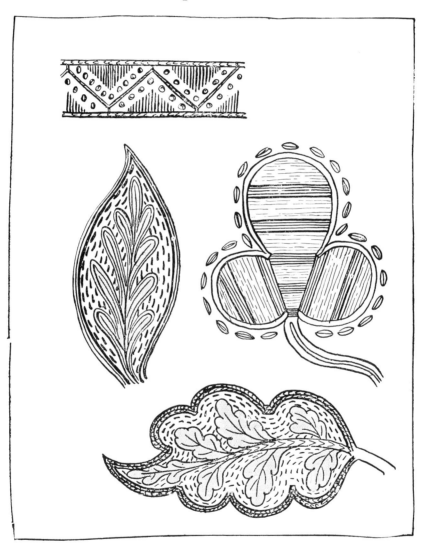

PLATE 14

Op. VI

HE following sketch was done from bed hangings, the property of the Earl of Powis, at Powis Castle.

PLATE 15

The design is a bold one of big leaves worked on the usual thick white hand-made linen. Undoubtedly the wools used were green at the time of working, but have now changed to beautiful shades of blue to indigo. Each leaf throughout the work has a thick contour in rope stitch of the four shades of the wool used, and the stem is most effective, done in squares of Cretan stitch in the same four shades.

Op. VI

PLATE 15

Op. VII

PLATE 16

THIS bold leaf is mainly carried out in block shading, but the colours are unusual. Indigo for the outside edge, soft brown the central block, and light green for the inner; in the second leaf the green is employed only for the line of veining; the two leaves or sections on the right-hand side are treated as follows—The upper one has outlines of brown, between which blocks of "buttonhole" in indigo are worked, the intervening spaces being simply decorated by a loop stitch in green wool. The sprays are in satin stitch, which is one of the best for small sprays to be worked solid.

PLATE 16

Op. VII

PLATE 17

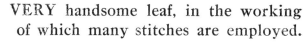 VERY handsome leaf, in the working of which many stitches are employed.

The curved scroll at the top is carried out in block shading in blue to pale green; the curved section on the right is marked out in squares filled alternately with satin stitches, with a simple French knot in each square, and by a square trellis secured in the centre by a cross stitch; the scroll below this is outlined in crewel stitch, and filled with laid work or strands of wool thrown across from edge to edge and couched by back stitches at the points of intersection.

The three leaves at the root of the stem are carried out in block shading in shades of grey green, the leaf above is outlined in crewel stitch and filled with fancy devices worked in buttonhole stitch with darning background; the centre motive is a solid mass of French knots, well raised and blue in colour. I have seen this same motive carried out in three shades, the lightest group at the point, the darkest at the back.

Op. VII

PLATE 17

Op. VII

PLATE 18

ORE fillings taken from a piece of work executed in the late 17th century.

I Is one of the diverse methods of treating the large tree stems in a design. Within the fan-like outlines traced down on the linen is a solid filling of satin stitches, varying row by row from pale fawn at the foot to dark chestnut brown round the top, the direction of the stitches is shewn in the drawing.

II Here we have a fancy lattice of three strands of laid wool couched with small French knots at the intersecting points, the outline is in stem stitch and fanciful back stitches are used as fillings.

III Has first rows of long single threads thrown across, caught down with stars and groups of satin stitching crossed.

IV A light treatment for stems, the filling, shells in buttonhole stitches, with second outline in darning.

V One of the examples of the introduction of lace stitches that is to be noted in work of the late 17th century, the alternate blocks are in basket stitch, the others in double cross stitch in contrasting colours.

VI Quaint example of couched work.

Op. VII

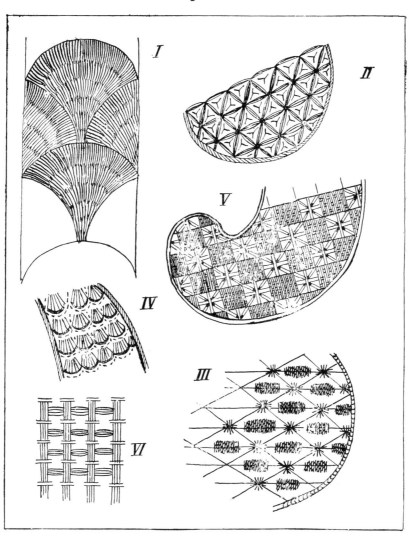

PLATE 18

Op. VII

PLATE 19

 A COLLECTION of particularly beautiful fillings seen in a Georgian copy of a very old example.

I Has double rows of outline stitch, framing spaces filled with stars in back stitch, the centre being solid in shading stitch.

II Outline of rope stitch and cross trellis of the same. Stars of back stitch couched down with contrasting wools.

III Part of a beautiful stem, outline of chain bars of button stitch in double wool and spots in loop stitch.

IV The two small petals filled solid with stem stitch, three rows of which are used for outlining the long petal, the centre being filled with rings in buttonhole stitch and darned background.

V Is carried out in satin and stem stitch, with back stitch bars couched with contrasting wool.

40

Op. VII

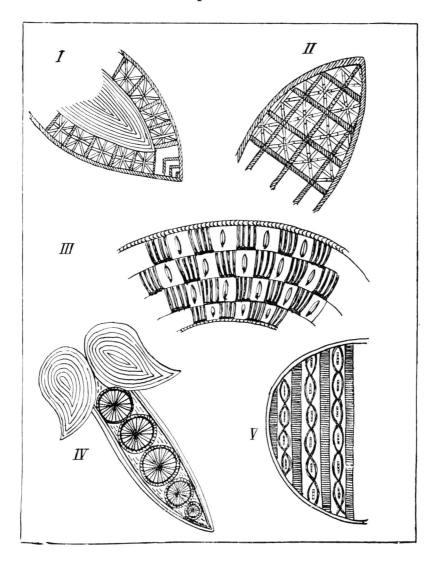

PLATE 19

Op. VIII

PLATE 20

THESE two sketches were taken from an 18th century (?) curtain done in solid, crewel work, in somewhat bright colouring. The brown veining which occurs in I and in nearly all the leaves was most effective; in this plate is also shown a good example of basket stitch stem work. The acorn cup was worked in close French knots.

II The large leaf is a good example of solid work. The contour was in stem stitch, the serrated edges turned over on to the brown surface were in shading stitch, the red veinings in satin stitch.

Op. VIII

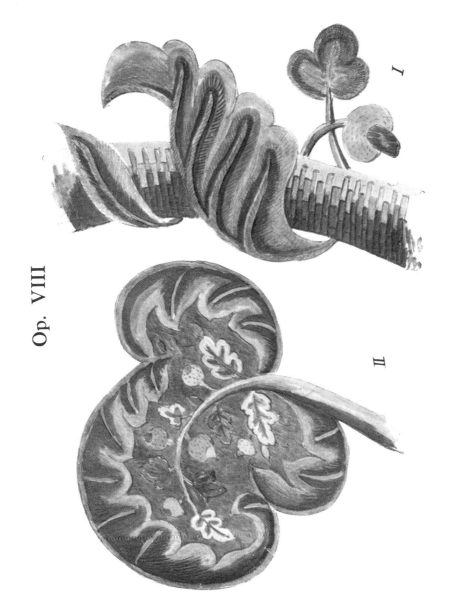

I

II

PLATE 20

Op. VIII

PLATE 21

THESE two leaves are of a bold, simple character that is easy to suggest, and proves a great relief in a design that is somewhat over-detailed. The large one is carried out in browns and greens. The turned over serrated edge is in satin stitch of graduating shade. The heavy veining is somewhat unusual in that it is carried out in laid stitch, dark green in the centre and light green outside. The stars are worked in dark green. The outline to the lower leaf is in two shades of green, the palest continuing to outline the remainder of the large leaf.

The small leaf is worked solid in shading stitch in blue with brown satin stitch edge, the veining is brown as is also the contour of the upper point.

Op. VIII

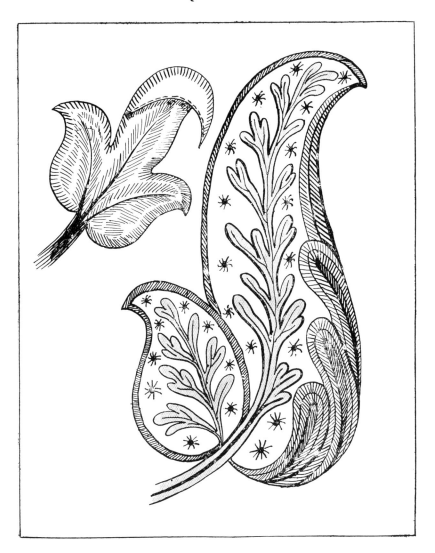

PLATE 21

Op. VIII

PLATE 22

WE have here a large leaf very characteristic of the complicated detail introduced by the conventional treatment of foliage in early English work.

The curved point of the leaf is outlined in rope stitch in a dark shade of soft bronze green, the heavy double cross lines are in crewel stitch and of a lighter shade of bronze in which the square lattice is also carried out, the French knots in the centres are of a dark olive green.

The round medallion is outlined similarly to the above but in darker shade, the centre being worked solid in slanting satin stitches set in rows, each row taken at the opposite angle to its neighbour; the next leaf is outlined inside, in two rows of chain, the turnover of the leaf being solid satin stitch in three shades of green. The stem is double back stitch, and the other leaves are worked solid in shading stitch in graduated shades of green.

The two small leaves, I & II example: 1st, rope stitch with alternate fillings of darning and outline stitch, and 2nd, rows of outline stitch for one-half the back leaves and one-half grey knot stitch and blue snail trail in alternative, the end leaf being in rows of outline of brown colour.

46

Op. VIII

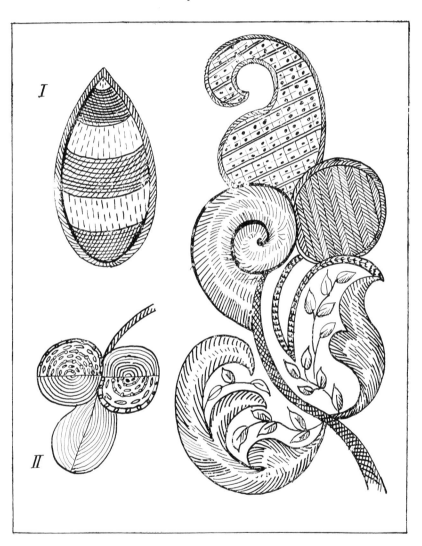

PLATE 22

Op. VIII

PLATE 23

A PORTION of the terra firma of the curtain.

The strawberries and clear parts of the ground are worked in French knots.

The plants are very useful in breaking up the solid masses of dark colour, and the stag serves to introduce into the base of the work the colouring of the acorns above (on plates 1 and 2).

As a rule this base of a design repeats all the colourings used throughout.

Op. VIII

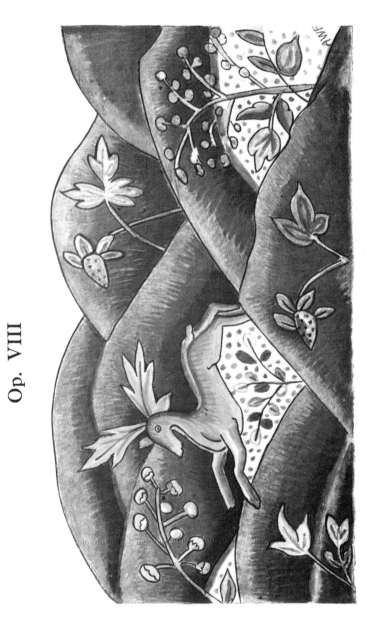

PLATE 23

Op. VIII

PLATE 24

EXAMPLE of a bird **introduced into the** late 17th century work.

It is executed in simple feather stitch for the tail feathers and satin stitch very evenly shaded. The dark centres of the short feathers are in crimson, the rest in shades of buff, the breast feathers also worked in satin stitch are in putty colour, legs and beak are brown and the crest in crimson.

Öp. VIII

PLATE 24

Op. VIII

PLATE 25

QUAINT early example of a parrot, head in knot stitch, breast feathers block stitch, and wings in shaded single feather stitching.

The butterfly and grub are found in all early examples.

Op. VIII

PLATE 25

Op. VIII

PLATE 26

GROUP of animals usually disporting on the terra-firma at base of large designs.

Worked always in long and short stitch.

Op. VIII

PLATE 26

Op. VIIl

PLATE 27

SQUIRREL in rich brown colour, with cream chest worked in shading stitch, tail in overcasting for the centre and furry part in single feather stitch with stem stitch outline.

Insect with brown body and blue wings veined black.

Op. VIII

PLATE 27